FIVE SE

CREATE A ~~STRESS~~ *BALANCED LIFESTYLE IN FIVE*

MINUTES A DAY

By Marta Tuchowska

Copyright © 2014, 2016
by Marta Tuchowska

TABLE OF CONTENTS

FROM THE AUTHOR

I always say that if you want to be successful (no matter what it is that you want to achieve), you must become committed to a holistic self-care plan, not only taking care of your body, but also your mind, emotions, and spirit. This is how you can create a stronger and more balanced version of yourself. However, remember this is not only about the final results. This is mostly about going through the process of a total body and mind transformation, as well as embracing all of the positive changes in yourself, your body, your reactions and all of your achievements. Rome wasn't built in a day, right?

It always distresses me when I see someone go on another fad diet and get too fixated on weight loss, instead of focusing on creating a healthy and nutritionally balanced lifestyle that works for them long-term. You see, everyone is different and my diet plan will never be the same in your case. It is just like how my meditation techniques will change when you get your beautiful hands on them. Everyone is different and unique, which is a wonder of life.

Many people learn about the benefits of meditation and immediately come up with pretty unrealistic goals like, *I will meditate for about 2 hours straight every day.* Sometimes even 30 minutes might be an unrealistic goal if you are new to it. Besides, forget about how much you meditate. Forget about all of those measurements and judgments. A good book is a good book. It doesn't matter if it has 2000 pages or 100 pages, just like a bad book will be a bad book for you, no matter how many pages it has.

This is going to be a journey and there will be bad moments as well. Still, if you want to make regular meditation your lifestyle and take care of your spiritual wellness, you will have to get committed to it. You will have to use your mind and just do it anyway, even if you don't feel like it. Such a simple rule, yet many people reject it and, therefore, ruin their healthy lifestyles (plus they sabotage themselves). A simple example, "I want to stop drinking alcohol, but I don't want to drink water while I am hanging out with my friends, who drink." Another good example is, "I want to change my nutrition, but I am not the kind of a person who makes green smoothies first thing in the morning" or "I really want to start working out, but it feels nicer to stay in and watch TV. Besides, I am tired today!" Lastly, "I need more fitness and weight loss motivation. I read about it, but I still need this extra push. It's the author's fault that I am not getting any results!"

Now I am not judging, I have been there myself. I would procrastinate about many things and would look for excuses. Since I committed myself to taking care of my body, mind and spirit, I do have a certain kind of routine that I stick to, even if I don't feel like it. Why? Because I am responsible for creating my lifestyle. I need to be proactive, not reactive. I think as an investor, not a consumer, this is why my life is changing. One simple decision can change your life, too. So get committed and take action, which in this case will be your regular meditation practice. Even a minute a day will do, if you are serious about it, and if you are reading this book, I assume you are. It's all about creating healthy habits that last.

Let's compare this concept to a diet again. Forget about counting calories and focus on quality nutrition and real foods. You see meditation is no different, my friend. It all comes down to putting your mind to it and making it your lifestyle. I very often meditate just for a few minutes when taking a break from writing; or I go for a short walk. It's all about fueling your mind and your spirit and connecting to what I call a Peaceful Warm Nourishing light. This is something that is always there for you to cheer you up and give you energy.

Do you want to feel relaxed on a physical level, yet energized mentally? Do this simple exercise, you can thank me later:

Sit down, lie down, or stand up, whatever feels right for you. You can even do it when you are walking. Take a few deep breaths and feel grateful that you have air to breathe. Breathe in and out of your nose, just like in yoga. Or breathe in your nose and out your mouth. You see, this is something that we take for granted and we are focusing on what we don't have instead of on what we have. I must admit that I often fall a victim of this pattern as well, and I need to remind myself the gift of gratitude and fulfillment. You see, I am not perfect. I am not a spiritual guru and I never said I was.

Back to our meditation-keep breathing like I suggested. You can also start breathing in and out your mouth, which is <u>a technique used in Reiki</u>. This is more difficult and you will need more focus to do this, but it's really calming and purifying. It also makes you leave your usual comfort zone, which is the way we normally breathe (through the nose, right?). Anyway, don't worry that much about which way of breathing you decide to employ. What is quite important though is to make your breathing deep and feel your belly moving as well, we want to use our diaphragm.

Now, imagine a big, white, warm light that is approaching you and surrounding your body as a shield. It makes you feel calm and protected. It smells of lavender (or vanilla, or fruits - choose whatever suits you) and makes you even more relaxed. If you are not walking, I suggest you close your eyes and tap them with your hands. Keep breathing and greet the White Light. Thank it for protection. Now imagine the light entering your body through your head. You can feel its pulsating energy spread throughout your body and it feels really nice. Keep visualizing and feeling. You see some people are more visual and some people prefer to feel instead of visualizing. In this book, we will be working on all your senses, but remember to stick with whatever it is that works for you and feels right. Though at the same time force yourself to leave the comfort zone and discover new things. Try them and embrace them. Reject them if they are not for you- you are the boss here.

As the light goes deep and deep into all your cells, you focus back on your breathing. Now you also breathe in the light and can feel it in your lungs. You are surrounded by the White Warm Light and so it is not possible for you to breathe in and absorb negativity, only positivity.

Now, open the palms of your hands and ask for more light that will be entering through your hands. Finally, imagine that the light is also underneath you and it makes you feel grounded and secure. It starts entering your body through your feet. As you keep breathing in, you are feeling more and more relaxed.

Now, the light also has an amazing smell and a gentle sound of a waterfall. You see, this light is like a waterfall of joy and it spreads throughout all your body. When you touch it with your hands it's warm and protective. Stay with the light as long as you need to. Try to do this a few times during the day and at least once before you proceed to reading this book. You have just done your first steps in the amazing Five Senses Healing Meditation. All you had to do was create your own protective light and make it work for you. Imagination and being gentle to yourself can work miracles for your spiritual wellness and overall well-being.

I believe that you need a really strong mind-spirit connection to create a healthy and vibrant body.

Since I have used the word "spirit," let me tell you what it means to me. Everyone can fill in the blanks here and tell me what it means for them. <u>The review section of this book</u> is also a great place to share your thoughts with the rest of the world.

For me, the spirit is the part of us that helps us become more fulfilled, happy and balanced. It helps us connect the intellectual mind with our emotions and make sure that we know how to become captains of our own ships.

I have been looking for a definition of spirituality for a really long time. I used to think that a spiritual person is someone who goes to church and has a deep faith in whatever religion they have chosen to follow. I used to think that a spiritual person is also someone who is a medium, has other psychic abilities, or who spends hours meditating, doing yoga or is vegan. Don't get me wrong - many people who fall into the above mentioned categories are spiritual, but not all of them. Also, I don't really like to use the word "category", just as I don't like classifying people. This is just to make my point clear, ok? Unfortunately, think about all the religious wars in human history. Were they spiritual?

You see, spirituality is about helping and understanding other people. It does not matter if you follow certain religions, or if you don't. It's not that I don't believe in religions, or that I criticize you or other people for following one. I think that religions were created to help people feel reunited with their White Warm Lights and help one another. Unfortunately, the human mind can be very deceitful sometimes and so it has decided to add ego, personal benefits and personal opinions that were supposed to work for everyone at the same time.

You see, I haven't figured out my religion yet, and what I personally find important for me is to <u>know my definition</u> of spirituality and stick to it. This is what I have been focusing on: creating my own vision of spirituality and spiritual wellness. I hope it can help you in your journey of personal fulfillment. Again, what you think may be different to what I personally believe in, which is the beauty of personal beliefs. Cultivate yours and respect other people and their beliefs. As long as your beliefs are not hurting anyone, I think you are good to go.

So...what is spirituality?

It was when I was in Italy in 2009, and a friend of mine told me, "A spiritual person is a person who is willing to help other people."

This guy, and his wife, actually helped me and sorted me out with a place to stay. Alongside other people whom I hardly knew, yet they were willing to help me... As opposed to those who would call themselves my "friends," or wanted to seem really "cool, spiritual people" (appearances), but would not move their finger when someone needed their help and attention. I don't want to sound judgmental, I am not perfect myself.

But this concept has changed my life. I started looking around and I saw many ordinary people who were actually highly spiritual - they just wanted to be there for other people. How do you become a spiritual person? Well, it's all about developing your empathy towards others and creating a balanced lifestyle that works for you so that you feel at peace. Meditation will help you become more spiritual.

What do you gain when you try to embrace spirituality?

Fulfillment is what most people on Earth are looking for. You see, Tony Robbins says, "Success without meaning is a failure." In other words, it's not how much you achieve, but how you achieve it. You must know where you're going.

Regular meditation practice does just that for you. It helps you reconnect with yourself, ask yourself questions (even if you are not aware of it) and create a clear and balanced vision for yourself and for your life.

I have wanted to write this book for a really long time, yet I felt petrified as I feared the possible judgment. This is why I was hiding behind my recipe books most of the time. Don't get me wrong, I am really passionate about healthy living, wellness and healthy recipes. You need to work on your body to build up a foundation of vibrant health and focused mind. But there is so much more to be done.

For many people taking care of their body may the end of their journey, (which is OK if this is what they choose for themselves) but for others, like me, this is the beginning. I am a seeker, a holistic researcher, and so are you because you are reading this book. This is what we have in common, my friend!

I always say that wellness is not about how many green smoothies you drink, how well you're doing with pilates or fitness, or how many hours you spend on your yoga mat. If you want real holistic wellness, there must be a long, lasting change. You must commit yourself to work not only on your body, but also on your mind and spirit.

I am fascinated by the power of the mind and how much a human being can learn and achieve; how we can unleash the hidden potential and unlimited motivation that we actually all possess. Very often, wellness is not created by what you know, but how you think and react. In other words, no amount of information on health and wellness (or whatever it is that you are pursuing - money, financial freedom, great relationships) will help if there is no ability to change your mindset and eradicate your limiting beliefs.

You need information, motivation, and inspiration. Plus, all systems must go - body, mind and spirit. This is what I try to convey through all my books, articles, courses and programs. Now, this is why my blog is called <u>Holistic Wellness Project</u>, and there is much more to be discovered there. While the body and physical health part are utterly important, we must not neglect the spirit and the mind part that will also result in emotional wellness.

Become **your own holistic coach**, and mindfully observe how a healthy body results in a balanced, focused mind and a fulfilled spirit. Work on your mind to create some new empowering habits and fight with your limiting beliefs. Get committed to leaving your comfort zone. You will notice that your soul and your essence, will feel even more fulfilled, as with a positively changed mindset you will be able to help more people. You will also have more tools to apply all the healthy techniques to work on your body. For example, I know people who know much more about wellness, fitness and naturopathy than I do. Yet, they always fall off track and this is because they refuse to work on their mind or find out WHY they fall off track. They are not persistent with achieving their health goals. They choose to collect new recipes instead, but no amount of recipes will help if you can't force yourself to make them your lifestyle. Sound familiar? We have all been there, right?

And now, that's the best part of holistic <u>nutrition</u>. By working on your essence and your spirit, you <u>nourish your body and mind</u>. This helps you become more mindful. You can control your emotions and create the best version of yourself. This is going to be a process, "the process," and your very own process. Look forward to it, as to an exciting journey that will conjure up a stronger version of yourself.

This is going to be what I call "active mindfulness", as we will be working with all the senses. I have been applying those techniques in my own life, as well as teaching them to my friends, family and clients. Of course, since everyone is different, everyone has different experiences with it, but we all agreed on the following:

- This kind of meditation makes you more aware and mindful of what you eat and it helps you **fight emotional eating** in an all natural way.
- You can utilize this form of meditation even in the busiest life. You can even use your commuting time and arrive to or from work feeling more relaxed.
- You can apply it to add to holistic pain management treatments.
- You feel more **empathy** towards others. Sometimes you even get on a "natural high" and things just flow. It is perfect before stressful situations when you need to regain your self-confidence and be assertive.
- You can use it in your office **to energize yourself**.
- You develop creativity and focus.
- You gradually **eliminate negative emotions** and negative beliefs.
- Plus, it's free and you can take it with you everywhere you go. Once you make it your lifestyle, it will always be with you and it will become automatic.

Now, like I said, this is going to be a journey, so you must be willing to take action and be persistent with it. Again - it's not how many hours or minutes a day you meditate, but it's more about creating your own rituals and enjoying them.

I really hope that you will feel excitement when reading this book and apply it to your life. The more you apply what I am trying to show you, the more positive changes you will see. Finally, you will experience the real holistic wellness and the body, mind and spirit connection. This is my wish for you.

One more thing - I am not telling you what to do. I am telling you what I do. Take what you want and reject the rest. I am not a guru, but a "do-ro". I only share what I have tested on myself and experienced personally. I encourage you to use my meditation strategies to come up with your own.

Finally, my beliefs may be different than yours, which is simply because we are all different. I will always respect your beliefs and your way of life. I am just asking you to respect mine. We are here to help each other. Honest feedback is one thing and I always appreciate it, but judgment is another. It is destroying all of us in the long term.

Having said that, I also must mention that I am not without blame. Judgment is so deeply ingrained in our minds that it's hard to get rid of it. We all have judged and we have been judged. It's like a vicious cycle that I personally try to break as much as I can. Of course, I am just a fragile human being, not a spiritual guru. I am on a journey that I want to share with you, the reader.

I encourage you to take notes while you're reading. If you happen to have any questions or reflections, you can always send me an e-mail. I love hearing from my readers and I always get back to them personally.

www.HolisticWellnessProject.com

Thanks again for taking an interest in my book. In appreciation, I would love to offer you **a free audio book**: "Mindfulness for Busy People" as well as guided Five Senses Meditation. They will help you get started on meditation and mindfulness!

DOWNLOAD LINK:

<u>www.holisticwellnessproject.com/mindfulness</u>

As an added bonus, I will also send you a free copy of my book "Holistically Productive" (PDF and MOBI formats).

Introduction

Create Your Own Holistic Temple

We are living in a crazy, crazy world. This statement is the most accurate way to depict how a modern man lives his life these days.

Nowadays, everyone seems to be moving at all times. Somehow, you've gotten this notion that, if you are important, then you must find yourself busy doing something at all times. It's a good thing to be productive and proactive; however, many people get too active, and very often reactive. There are always deadlines that you need to meet. And once you've met those deadlines, there would always be another task waiting to be completed. You live in a world where life seems to be a never ending checklist of things to do and things to accomplish. But where is the fulfillment and real happiness? Where is the meaning? Where is the spirit part?

You are blazing and running through life doing everything that you can to cross out one task after another, in the soonest time possible. You race against someone else, against time and, at times, against yourself. Life around you becomes a blur of things to do and faceless people. You've lost touch and connection with the people and things around you, and most of all, with yourself. Whereas, if you really want to be happy and fulfilled, you should make it all about you and commit yourself to holistic self-care.

Now, I am not telling you to get lazy. I just want to show you how you can carry on your projects in a proactive way by taking care of your body, mind, and spirit. You see, we all pursue our goals (I, myself, am a very goal-oriented person), because we believe that, thanks to our achievements, we will feel happier. However, with the power of meditation, we can experience all those emotions in just a few seconds. <u>It all comes down to gratitude and discovering a little kid inside you.</u>

You can feel good, happy and fulfilled right now, and guess what - if you give yourself that gift and make it your lifestyle, you will start attracting more and more good things into your life. Even if you don't believe in the Law of Attraction, think about it as "Law of Action"- you take action and you decide to feel good. Now, most people will be naturally attracted to you and your energy. You will see that things will flow, and there will be less stress.

Amidst the chaos, confusion and disorder, have you ever had that nagging feeling in the gut that maybe, just maybe, there is another way that you can live your life? One that is still, peaceful and mindful? A life that will allow you to feel, to relish and to appreciate every experience and every moment to the fullest? You don't need to wait till your vacation or your retirement or until the unexpected happens...

How do you stop moving? How do you stand still and remain calm amidst the noise and storms that are constantly plaguing you? How do you stay grounded and connected to those that really matter? How do you allow yourself to feel alive? Or maybe...can you keep moving and yet be still?

Keep in mind that before you got caught up in this whirlwind that you now call "life", you were once all these. You were still and calm. You were grounded and connected. You were feeling everything. You were living life. You just got busy, preoccupied and overwhelmed trying to survive life that you forgot what it is like to actually live life. You began postponing your life, but health and emotions can never be neglected. Neither can your spirit that wants to work for you and make you feel grounded and focused.

So here I come, trying to help you remember what it's like to be mindful and aware of life as it happens inside and around you. I want to remind you how beautiful life is and how much joy and happiness you can find in it. This book will lead and guide you as you find your way back to life, love, joy and happiness in just a few simple steps that everyone can take.

By the way, this book is both for beginners, as well as those who are not new to meditation. Personally, I don't think that we can classify those who meditate as "beginners" or "advanced", after all - how can you measure one's progress in meditation? Their results? How many hours they have meditated? How they look? How they talk? You see, when it comes to meditation, we are all on the same level really. I can learn from you and you can learn from me.

Let's make it a judgment free zone as much as possible, ok? And yes, this book is for everyone and everyone can benefit from what I am sharing here.

What is Meditation?

The best way to understand meditation is to first look at the literal meaning of the word itself. The word meditation originated from the Latin word *meditari*, which simply means *to think*. This simple definition right away demystifies the most common misconception that many people have towards meditation: that it is all about leaving the mind blank, being in a seemingly catatonic state, not seeing, thinking or feeling anything at all. This misconception very often stops people from meditating as they reject it as "this is not for me," or "I find it hard." Our minds can get funny sometimes and they can even prevent us from achieving emotional and spiritual wellness. It's up to us if we decide to train them in a proactive way.

So, if you have ever heard "meditation is boring," or "meditation is not for everyone," or "it's not possible to just sit still," reject them. These are purely misconceptions, limiting beliefs and not true at all. In fact, meditation is nothing but work. Just like yoga is, because apart from physical and mental muscles, we also need to work on your emotional and spiritual muscles and make sure we strive for progress and balance.

Meditation is a practice that actually trains the mind to achieve a certain level of consciousness in order to achieve physical, emotional and spiritual benefits. Meditation can even be the end goal itself. Meditation propels the mind to be aware of the present moment and all the things that are happening in it. It teaches us how to be honest with ourselves and it brings a person's awareness, consciousness and senses to the here and now. By doing so, one is allowed to experience, delight and take pleasure in the sights, smell, taste, sound and feel of everything that is going on in the present moment. All these, are contrary to the myth that meditation leaves the mind blank and empty of thoughts. You can meditate when you shower, eat, walk around and listen to music. It's totally up to you. It's not about spending hours in a lotus pose on your yoga mat - of course, there is nothing wrong with this approach, but I guess that as a modern, busy person, you would not find time for that. Hence, you would give up on the whole process of learning how to meditate.

When meditating, a person's mind is actually elevated in a state of perpetual alertness and deep focus. It is able to tune out all the distractions, noise and static of a busy life. It can remain and it can allow itself to enjoy, acknowledge and feel the present moment and every emotion and feeling that go with it, without judgment and attachment.

Achieving a meditative state is not always easy. Not everything that is in the here and now is happy and beautiful. There might be pain and sadness. Accept it as this is how you are going to get stronger. There might be suffering and fear. It takes a lot of commitment, courage and heart for a person to be able to face and acknowledge the present moment. Facing the here and now with the help of meditation makes it a bit easier. Meditation helps prepare the body, mind and soul to acknowledge and accept the present moment and everything that goes with it with an attitude of openness and gratefulness, allowing a person in the end, to relish in the beauty of what is real and true. Sometimes, it's not about changing the world and pretending that white is black or black is white. Sometimes, it's about <u>changing your perception</u> of what is happening around you and learning how to reach the truth and learn from every experience that you encounter - both good and bad.

Meditation and the Five Senses

There are many types of meditation that are being practiced these days. There are meditations that focus on creativity and concentration. There are also meditations that that focus on awareness, attentiveness and awakening of one's energy centers in the body.

One type of meditation that stands out from the rest is what many call Five Senses Meditation, which is what I personally really love to practice as much as I can. This is a simple and beautiful meditation practice that allows you to explore and experience your sense of self by engaging your five senses to savor and relish the present moment and everything that comes with it. I am a big fan of simplicity and making things easy - life can be complicated enough and we oftentimes tend to make things more complicated than they really are.

We humans have five sensory organs that we should be really grateful for. Every day I say "thanks" to the Universe for all of them, especially for my eyesight. You see, I have suffered from a really serious eye condition that could have resulted in blindness. This is why I see eyesight as something we can't take for granted. Yet, so many people take stuff for granted and focus on what they don't have (even the richest people in the world will always find something they don't have!). They

21

focus on what they don't have, <u>instead of drawing our attention to what we actually have.</u>

We have our eyes to see, our nose to smell, our ears to hear, our tongue to taste and our skin to feel. It is believed that a state of meditation can be achieved when harmony and union is achieved among all the five senses. When our senses are still and in harmony with one other, we are able to quiet our mind and acknowledge the beings that we truly are. When our senses are in harmony, everything around us achieves a higher level of clarity. We begin to see, hear, smell, taste and feel in a more mindful and truthful manner. We allow ourselves to actually hear the callings of our soul and of the Universe itself.

I personally have three natural ways to lift me up and feel connected:

1. Music
2. Nature
3. Physical Activity

   Or all of them at once – I can go for a walk in nature, listen to music and...admire what I encounter on my way. I try to reconnect with the kid inside me.

In this type of meditation, our five senses connect us to the Self and to the Universe. Our five senses are constantly absorbing impressions from the world around us. These impressions are then forever imprinted within us. Finding a way to harmonize and unify our senses will allow us to bring balance in our lives and, again, this can be achieved even in a few seconds, if you put your mind to it.

When we use our senses to achieve a meditative state, we are able to acknowledge that the use of our senses goes beyond simple physical stimuli. We begin to understand their true value in our lives. These senses are more than physical organs. They are, in fact, vital in our growth as spiritual beings.

During the act of meditation, the use of our five senses can help us realize that the impressions and experiences we absorb from everything around us through our five senses are crucial in our quest to nurture and cultivate ourselves.

Meditation through the five senses helps us achieve a higher level of relaxation. In this state, we begin to see beyond what we simply see, hear beyond what we usually hear, taste more than we can actually taste, smell more than what we can normally smell and feel much deeper than what we usually feel. We begin to understand that beyond these stimuli is the Divinity in all things around us. We begin to discover the true meaning of things around us. We begin to understand what life is all about. We are able to actually feel and live life without being scared and apprehensive. We embrace every second of life. We begin to understand that what our senses absorb are beyond simple stimuli. They lead us to a much more aware state where we get to experience and delight in what is real and true.

The successive chapters of this book will guide you as make use of your five senses in finding a way back to your Self and to life itself. It will become your personal meditation guide and it will walk you through each step with candidness and mindfulness. It will be taking you through each step with gentle reminders and easy instructions. This book will not give you complicated theories and jargons that you will find hard to understand and comprehend. I want to keep it easy so that you feel more motivated and start applying whatever it is that suits you most. If, in the process of discovering a new, more mindful and focused version of yourself, you create your own way of meditating, please share it with other readers in the review section of this book. Let's help one another. After all, it's all about creating your way, right?

This book is written for you by someone who - like you - has also gone through life searching and looking for balance, peace and happiness. She had looked in many places, had tried many things, but forgot one thing. You see, she forgot to look in the one place where she should have looked first. She forgot to look within her to find that the answers to her questions have been there all along. All she needed was to make use of the gifts that she already had. Mindfulness and gratitude go hand in hand.

As you go through this book, keep an open mind and let the new learning take you to where you've always wanted your life to be. All these will be revealed to you in time as you, slowly, begin to make use of the five senses that were bestowed upon you.

Enjoy this book. Marvel at the wonders and beauty that you already have. Let it take you back to the life and the person that you once have been — balanced, peaceful, grounded and true.

CHAPTER 1

Discover All Your Senses and Feel Rejuvenated in Just a Few Seconds

Have you ever wondered where our feelings of anxiety and depressions are coming from? Most of the time, these feelings are not actually about ourselves, but rather about the things that are NOT happening to us at the present moment. There are times when we find ourselves nostalgically drifting towards the past, longing for things to go back to the way they used to be.

There are also moments when we find ourselves fussing and worrying over what would happen in the future. We are everywhere, but here. We say that the grass is always greener on the other side of the fence, or somewhere else, but not where we actually are. We are waiting for the unexpected to happen. We have traveled back in time and into the future, but have never managed to remain in the present moment. We have become restless souls, always searching, always looking, and never standing still.

How then, do we break away from this fatal cycle of restlessness? The answer is quite simple, my friend. Meditate. Be aware that you are here, now, and find peace in the process. This does not mean that you have to sit still or look very calm physically. Personally, I have met many people who seemed to be really focused and calm from the outside, but they would admit that deep inside they were lost and torn. At the same time, I have met people who seemed active, always moving around and sometimes expressing their anger straight away, but deep inside they had their peace of mind. As they say - *don't judge the book by the cover*.

Be present. This is the core message of the practice of meditation. It seems like an easy task, but can be quite challenging to achieve. Let me challenge you now. Put this book down, close your eyes and allow yourself to be the king (or queen) of your castle.

Breathe in and out the way you feel is right for you. Keep telling your subconscious mind, "I am in control. I control how I feel. My emotions work for me." It's up to you how much time you decide to devote to this process. I always find it really energizing and uplifting, and just like yoga stretches that allow me to move and feel my body, this meditation reminds me that I create my own feelings. I like to repeat this process a few times a day (just like yoga poses). Short sessions, but repeated throughout the day, do wonders for my well-being and they help me develop new, empowering habits. Besides, I never get bored when going through this process and I never stress out thinking I don't have time.

You don't even have two minutes for the most important meeting today? The meeting with yourself? Then, how come you can be prepared for other meetings with your bosses, colleagues, employees, clients, family and friends..? If you want to be changing the world and maybe impress/help other people, you must first impress/help yourself. In order to achieve it, you must become a master of self-care. The master of self-care!

Mindfulness is the heart of the practice of meditation. This is the act of consciously bringing your awareness to the present moment without judgment and attachment. When you are mindful, you are going through each moment with a heightened awareness of your surroundings, thoughts, feelings and bodily sensations. Using your five senses, together with your breath, to bring awareness to the present moment, is one of the easiest ways to achieve a mindful state. There are no mantras to chant or difficult postures to perform. Of course, you can always explore them later, down the road. Meditation is a life-long study.

Meditating using your five senses it the most literal way to direct your consciousness to the present moment. It can effortlessly bring you to a relaxed state. Once you find yourself in a relaxed state, you can gently and easily quiet your mind. A quiet and still mind allows you listen to the callings of your heart, soul and the Universe. It can propel you to a higher level of consciousness and awareness that is shared with the Divine.

Discover all your senses by going through this simple and easy guided meditation:

Let us begin by finding a comfortable seating position. You can sit on a half or full lotus position, if you are familiar with the pose, or you can simply cross your legs. We are not looking for a perfect asana or posture here. What matters is that you are comfortable with your back straight.

Lift the crown of your head towards the heavens while grounding your sit bone to the earth. Feel your spine lengthening. Your neck is soft and long. Feel proud of yourself, you are taking one of the most important steps on your spiritual journey. You are discovering yourself. You deserve it.

Find openness in your chest. Feel your lungs expanding. Feel the rush of the air going through your nostrils. Breathe in through the nose and exhale through your nose. Find a rhythm as you feel the air going in and out of your body. Let it caress you like gentle waves in the ocean rocking you gently. Simply observe without judgment how your breath goes back and forth until you feel your muscles begin to relax. Unclench your jaw. It's unbelievable how much tension can accumulate there and in your throat chakra. Relax your face and your eyelids. Relax the soles of your feet. Let you body find rest in the gentle lull of your breath. Squeeze your eyebrows a few times to get rid of tension; it's like a gentle self-massage. Using all your fingers, massage your forehead - again, we tend to accumulate way too much tension than we can handle.

Now that you are relaxed, we will begin our journey to discover your senses. You are safe here. This is where you belong. Rest assured that your body is protected. You can let go. Allow your mind and soul to travel and flow freely.

See. You are on a beach. You are standing on the shore and gently gazing out to the horizon. You don't need to stare and strain your eyes. Simply let your gaze fall gently towards the horizon of the ocean. Be aware of its vastness and the distance spanned by the horizon. Notice the enormity of the ocean right before you. Don't feel overwhelmed, don't be afraid. Enjoy it and relax in it.

Slowly, dip into the waters and begin to float towards the horizon. Don't chase it relentlessly. Simply allow yourself to lightly float towards it. There is no pressure to reach it. You are simply unhurriedly, gently and quietly moving towards the horizon.

Hear. As you effortlessly float towards the horizon, you bring your awareness to the sound of water sloshing around you as you continue to float towards the horizon. You then become aware of the sound of the waves gently crashing into the shore. You can hear the bubbles fizzle as the waves break. You can hear the waters receding back into the vastness of the ocean. You listen to waves once again lapping on the shore. It goes back and forth, and slowly, you find yourself falling into its unique rhythm. It becomes your lullaby as the waves gently rock you to a peaceful slumber.

Feel. You were about to fall asleep when you suddenly find yourself washed ashore. You feel the wet sand on your face. You feel it's grittiness on your palms as you push yourself up and turn your body over. Finally, you are now lying on your back. You can still feel the wet and cold sand underneath you, but this time, you are also savoring the warmth of the sun as it gently shines down on you. You allow the sun to bathe you in its warmth. You feel your clothes slowly drying up.

As the sun continues to shine down on you, you decide to get up and walk towards the island. You are barefoot, but you don't mind. You like the feel of the find sand on your feet and on your toes. They tickle you a little bit, but you're okay with that. Sand walking massages your feet in an all natural way. You feel like you're at the most luxurious SPA there is!

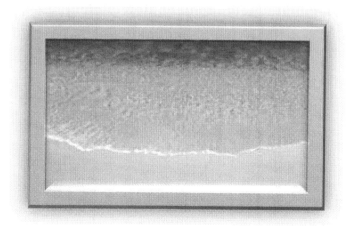

Be aware of how solid the ground is beneath you, even when you feel your feet leaving footprints on the sand. Be conscious of the feeling of stability that the earth brings you and continue walking.

Smell. As you keep on walking, you become aware of a sweet, fragrant smell coming from the woods that stand right before you.

You decided to follow the sweet scent and you make your way through the thicket and undergrowth, until you find yourself in a clearing. In the middle, is a small patch of rose bushes. The flowers are in full bloom and you find yourself filling your lungs with their sweet smelling scent.

The fragrance of the roses fills your soul with renewed vigor. You feel rejuvenated and invigorated after swimming for so long in the ocean.

You go from one flower to another, gently smelling them. You are in no rush because you know that you can always go back to them. The roses are like a gift of life. They renew your spirit and ask for nothing in return.

Taste. While you continue to explore the small garden you found in the middle of the clearing, you begin to feel hunger from swimming and walking for so long. Your hunger pulls you away from the roses and towards the small cottage at the edge of the clearing. You are able to allow yourself to easily leave the roses behind because you know that their sweet fragrance will last forever in your soul. You will never forget them. Your soul will always remind you of their sweet and aromatic smell whenever you need to rejuvenate.

You walk towards the cabin until you reach the front door. You slowly open the door and you are greeted by the most delectable aroma of food. There is soup boiling on the stove on the far corner of the cabin. The long table in the middle is laden with different kinds of healing foods. Before you is a feast fit for a king and queen...

You slowly make your way towards the table. You sit and start eating. You are mindful of each bite you take. You enjoy eating tropical fruits and other natural treats from Mother Earth. You see to it that you are eating slowly, enjoying and savoring each scrumptious meal. You are careful not to stuff your mouth with different kinds of food all at the same time. You allow yourself to take one bite at a time. You chew the food thoroughly until it begins to melt in your mouth. You take pleasure in every bite you take. The next bite is always more scrumptious than the last one. You do this with the other food on the table, until you find yourself full and sated.

After your meal, you look around you and see the bedroom. You walk towards it and gently open the door. Inside is a huge bed with soft pillows and warm blankets. You lie on it and rest. You are nourished, rejuvenated, warm and safe. You let your head fall gently on the pillow made of feathers and, slowly, you close your eyes.

Your journey has ended. You rest your body, knowing tomorrow will be another adventure. You will receive new gifts, you will witness new sights, you will taste more delectable food, you will gain new experiences and life will be much richer. But for now, you rest and allow yourself to relish in the triumphs of today.

When you cultivate and bring focus to your five senses, you are able to unite them. When your senses are in harmony, you allow your body to experience a deeper state of meditation that you deserve.

CHAPTER 2

Focus On Your Vision and Discover How Beautiful the World is: Be the Master of Your Own Reality

Let us begin the process of nurturing and cultivating your five senses with your sense of sight.

Your eyes allow you to glimpse reality. What you see can alter your perception of what is real and true. Nurturing this will help widen your perception and allow you to see beyond physical stimuli.

Before we begin, keep in mind that the objective in this exercise is to bring awareness and mindfulness into the present moment by using your sense of sight. We are not going to change, force or chase anything. We are simply letting things be.

When going through meditation with focus on your vision, you must also remember that you will continue to feel, smell, taste and hear things. Don't be bothered by that. Don't consider these other sensations as distractions. Just let them be. You just have to gently remind yourself that, this time, your focus and attention will be only on things that you see.

Let us begin by allowing yourself to relax. Find a comfortable sitting position. You can also do it when walking, it's up to you. The location does not really matter as long as you are comfortable with it. The goal in this exercise is to allow yourself to see beyond what you can see. To find beauty in all things, no matter what the circumstances may be.

Bring your attention to your breath. Observe the rise and fall of your chest as the air goes in and out of your body. Don't try to manipulate and control your breath. Don't try to prolong and hold it. Let it flow freely and allow your breath to travel all over your body. As you slowly find yourself drifting towards a certain state of calmness and stillness, begin to shift your awareness to what is in front of you. Ask yourself what you can see all around you. Notice what they are. Don't judge. Simply state what they are.

Let us take for example a vase with a single flower in it. Let us say this is what you saw in front of you upon opening your eyes. Pay attention to its shape and color. Notice how the color changes with the light. Visualize the rays of the sun as it softly bounces from the smooth surface of the face, giving you that shimmering and glittering reflection. Gently trace with your eyes the contours of each petal. Notice how they move ever so slightly as the wind gently blows through it. Using your sense of sight, pay attention to the smooth and shiny texture of the vase. Notice how it complements the soft texture of the petals.

As you take in every detail that you see, be mindful of your reactions. Notice how you respond to every observation that you take in. Did the color remind you of something? Did it trigger an emotion deep within you? Did it stir up a long forgotten memory? Did it give you feelings of hope and anticipation?

No matter how you react to what you saw, gently remind yourself not to judge those reactions. Simply observe those feelings rise up and die down. Don't try to control them. Don't feel bad about yourself either for having those emotions or thoughts toward the object that you are seeing. Simply accept that they were there, at the present moment. Acknowledge their presence and let them dissipate on their own.

Finish the meditation by slowly closing your eyes and keeping them closed for about a minute.

Now, if you are up for an extra exercise, play some gentle music in the background and allow yourself to travel to amazing places that fill your heart and soul with joy. Allow your mind to create the best landscapes that make you feel peaceful. Capture those images; all of them, including those that were conceived by your imagination, those you saw in your dreams and those you saw in the real life.

Another thing that you can do, anytime and whenever you want, is to observe colors around you. Then, imagine that your eyes can make the tones more vibrant and appealing. Attach positive emotions to them and pin the images in your mind. You can easily create more relaxation for you in just a few minutes.

CHAPTER 3

Focus On What You Hear Around You and Create Amazing Sounds that Rejuvenate Your Body, Mind and Soul

Cultivating your sense of hearing allows you to eventually hear the callings of your heart, your soul and the Universe. The sounds of nature are the best music therapy. You can also attach sounds to colors and visual images - for example, green or green trees can sound like birds and the gentle wind, whereas, blue and blue ocean can sound like seagulls, waves and freshness... Can you see how the senses began to work together, overlap and create new, amazing realities full of beauty and fulfillment?

When you are mindful of the sounds that you hear, you learn how to uncover their different layers. You learn how to actually listen and pay attention. Eventually, you won't need to see things to know what they are. By simply listening to their sounds, you will know their true nature. You can feel emotions (yours and other people's) by simply listening.

Begin by once again bringing yourself to a relaxed state. The use of breathing as guide in this meditation is crucial. You can use it as your guide when you find yourself and your thoughts wandering somewhere else. Use it to pull you back to the present moment. Let it bring you back to the here and now.

Observe every inhalation and exhalation. Listen to the sound that you make every time the air goes in and out of your nostrils. Notice that every breath you take is full of life -giving oxygen that rejuvenates your blood and your cells. You may even begin to hear your heart beating. Notice that every beat, you are pumping out blood to all parts of your body. Acknowledge that the sounds you hear inside you are indications and affirmations of the life that you've been blessed to have, right at this very moment. While listening to your breath and your heartbeat, slowly shift your focus to the noise and sound around you. Try to unravel the different layers of sounds in your environment. Listen to the wind gently blowing in your face. Listen to the chirping of the birds. Listen as they flap their tiny wings. Even if you hear around you nothing but cars passing by, don't regard them as noise or distraction. Listen to their rhythm. Listen to the power of their engines. Listen how all these sounds come together and form some kind of music. Find the beat of life in the sounds that surround you.

Even if there is nothing but silence all around you, gently try to listen closely and you will hear something. Silence can tell you a lot of thing, if only you will allow it to talk to you and tell you its secrets. You will be amazed at the many things that it can reveal to you.

As you listen to the sounds around you, observe the various feelings that they evoke in you. Notice the sounds that appeal to you. Identify which sounds trigger a certain memory. Acknowledge the thoughts and emotions that are stirred up by these sounds. Don't chase them away. Don't judge and don't get attached either. Just allow these feelings to flow through you. Let them be, and, when the time is right, let them go.

What I really enjoy is "silence meditation", and ever since I discovered it, I get up early every day. Why? Because everything is so silent around me and I just like listening to silence and my own breath. This is when I find it easier to detect different, far away layers. For example, my neighbor's dog barking or an occasional car passing by, but since I live in really tranquil surroundings, this is pretty uncommon.

When I am really tired, I use music therapy to relax. It feels amazing to close your eyes and simply decide to focus on sounds, nothing else. It helps fight stress and refuels your mind. If you tend to think too much, or just feel tired after work, try to float away with your favorite sounds.

CHAPTER 4

Focus On Your Touch:

Discover the Power of Mindful Self-Massage Meditation and Relax in just a Few Minutes

A touch can heal and comfort the sick. It can soothe a tired and weary body. It can relieve pain and tension. A gentle touch can show someone love and compassion. A single touch can make a big difference in the lives of many people, and even the world!

To cultivate the power of your touch, we will give ourselves some loving through meditation and a relaxing self-massage. I am a big fan of self-massage with aromatherapy oils (that is, essential oils diluted in some cold-pressed base oil). This is what I always try to teach through all my books, courses and programs. You don't need to spend tons of money at your local spa, you can create your own spa at your home or office. You decide when you wish to relax, right?

Moreover, you want to make it your lifestyle - this is why you want to learn how to prevent stress from knocking on your door to begin with. Just like you brush your teeth or have a shower - you want to maintain a clean body and you don't even think about it, it becomes automatic. And so should be your commitment to a stress-free life. Stress-free does not mean lazy.

I like my active lifestyle, but I also want balance in my life. I know that by scheduling at least a few minutes a day for the most important meeting, the meeting with my boss - myself and I - I take care of my body, mind and spirit. While certain amounts of stress are good as they motivate us to achieve things and to be active and grow the border line between what we can call "acceptable stress" and stress that can take its toll on our emotions, health, and everyday life, is really thin. Prevention is the best medicine.

In one of my books on the alkaline diet and lifestyle (free download at: www.bitly.com/AlkalineMarta), *I mention that the alkaline lifestyle is not only about what you eat. It's also about what you think and how you live. Stress is acidic and harmful. Learning how to reduce it is as important as a healthy and balanced holistically nutritional plan.*

If you want, you can begin this meditation by listening to the sounds of the ocean, there are many amazing ocean sounds playlists on YouTube. Of course, this is optional, but why not treat yourself to some amazing exotic holiday right now? Your imagination can take you there and you will feel so relaxed.

Begin by bringing yourself to a relaxed state with the help of your breath. Breathe in through your nose and out through your mouth. Make it slow and deep. You need to breathe in the positive energy and let your body get rid of all kinds of toxins (mental, physical, emotional and spiritual). Once you find yourself in a relaxed state, visualize yourself in a white sand beach. Picture yourself lounging on a towel, underneath a coconut tree. Despite the shade of the tree, you can still feel the rays of the sun filtering through it. The sun warms you and you savor the feeling all throughout.

You are aware that as the day progresses, the sun's rays will burn you. So you reach out for a bottle of coconut sun block lotion. You squeeze out the cool and soothing lotion on the palm of your hand. You rub both hands together and gently begin to spread the lotion on your neck as you continue to sunbathe.

Begin by applying the lotion gently along the edge of your scalp. Apply small and gentle pressure as you trace the various pressure points along the scalp.

You can make small circles using your fingers as you continue to trace the edge of your scalp in long, sweeping motions. Focus on the occipital bone, there are many pressure points there and by working on them you can alleviate neck pain. Work on the hairline and your middle hair part. It's really, really easy and you don't need to become a master of acupressure to learn the basics.

From the scalp, gently apply pressure on your jaw lines while tracing its contours. Then, slowly, bring your fingers at the base of your skull. This is the nape of your neck. Work these areas by gently massaging it with the tip of your fingers. Be mindful of the pressure. Find one that feels good. The goal here is to release the tension in the neck. Continue doing these in light, but steady pressure until you feel the muscles of your neck slowly relaxing. After giving your neck a well-deserved massage, gently pull and massage your ears. Doing this further releases tension related to headaches and even migraines. This is really relaxing and therapeutic.

Once are you done massaging your ears, lay flat on your back, hug your knees to your chest and rock your body from side to side. Feel the tension from the entire length of your cranial sacral system (from your head to your tailbone) dissipate and evaporate.

Savor the light and liberating feeling of a body that is free from stress and tension. Close your eyes for a minute and bathe in the warmth of the sun shining down on you. Feel connected to the earth, as you surrender your back to the ground. Relax and enjoy.

I strongly encourage you to create your own self-massage rituals. Aromatherapy and essential oils will help you take your mindfulness meditation to the next level, and in the next chapter, I am going to show you how to meditate with aromatherapy oils. Create your own holistic spa whenever and wherever you want.

Looking for holistic self-care solutions on a busy schedule?

Download your free copy of my audiobook (read by the author): "Mindfulness for Busy People":

www.holisticwellnessproject.com/mindfulness

CHAPTER 5

The Power of Smell:

All You Need to Know about Mindful Aromatherapy Meditation

Get Hooked on the Pleasure of Aromatherapy - Unwind in Just a Few Seconds!

They say that certain smells can be powerful memory triggers. Researchers and scientists alike say that the nerves responsible for the sense of smell are located closely to the nerves responsible for our memories. This proximity between the nerves is believed to be one reason why our sense of smell is tied to our memories. Whenever we smell something, we have to recall when we have smelled it before. After that, we try to connect it to a picture or visual information, allowing us to eventually identify the scent.

To develop your sense of smell, we will go through meditation with aromatherapy oils. I personally found it hard to meditate and focus on meditation. This is why I would just say, "Meditation is not for me", and so I would stay in my comfort zone. Still, as a nervous person by nature, I knew that meditation would be one of the best natural therapies for me. It wasn't until I discovered aromatherapy that things began to change and I was actually looking forward to every aroma-meditative moment.

Aromatherapy makes it a lot easier for those who say they can't focus or find meditation boring. If you are one of them - use essential oils and focus your attention on scents. Close your eyes, you will see that the rest will come. Try this and, with only 5 minutes a day, you will discover how amazing it is for your overall health and wellness. If you are like me, or maybe you are not a very visual person, make sure you commit yourself to aromatherapy meditation. Actually, it will commit itself to serving you, 24/7, as long as you do it at least 5 minutes a day. Trust me!

Breathing is one of the core components of the practice of meditation. Using aromatherapy to further relax the body can help you easily achieve a meditative state, allowing you to find peace and stillness amidst the chaos and noise of your day to day life. Sound easy? Well it is, plus. Plus, it is really, really nice for all your senses, not only for the smell, and you are just about to discover why.

Aromatherapy stimulates the parasympathetic nervous system that, to simplify, helps us feel good and experience positive emotions and sensations. At the same time, it slows down the sympathetic nervous system that gets stimulated whenever we feel stressed out. Perfect combination for us! This is a free, 100% natural, holistic service that aromatherapy offers us.

Before meditating, choose the essential oil that will best suit your mood and your purpose. Essential oils have certain therapeutic and beauty properties - usually the same for everyone. However, as far as emotional and spiritual benefits are concerned, I believe these will differ according to a person. When meditating with essential oils, use scents that **serve your purpose**. I am going to list a few oils that are generally used for meditation purposes, as well as a few essential oils that I am personally a big fan of and use every day. However, it's all up to you - choose the oils that suit you, everyone is different.

Remember to use pure, organic and chemotyped oils. If you happen to have any questions about essential oils, email me at info@holisticwellnessproject.com, or check out my blog: www.holisticwellnessproject.com/blog/natural-therapy-spa/

You can use essential oils (EO) in a vaporizer, or add a few drops to your bath. If you are going for the second option, I suggest you mix them with a tablespoon of good quality base oil, for example avocado, olive, coconut or sweet almond oil - just to make sure that your skin doesn't get irritated. It would spoil the whole aromatherapy fun.

Another way is to mix a few drops of your chosen essential oil with some vegetable oil and go for aromatherapy massage. Coconut oil is great for that, you can also use sweet almond oil, kernel oil, hazelnut oil or whatever quality base oil you have. Don't use commercial, mineral oils. Massage yourself using aromatherapy blends while you meditate. My book: "Aromatherapy Recipes" covers the topic of blending oils for specific purposes, in case you want to learn more about it.

However, for now, you only need to know the basics and get committed to making aromatherapy meditation a part of your lifestyle. I am sure you will love it and your quality of life will improve. Your family and friends will be curious to find out what it is that you do to feel and look *SO amazing*.

HOW TO BLEND OILS FOR MASSAGE

Used by *the English School of Aromatherapy,* which is an approach that is usually employed in holistic spas.

1 tablespoon of vegetable oil (15ml) with 6-7 drops of essential oil(s)

Make the blend weaker when working on your face, or if you have really sensitive skin, especially if you are using essential oils like basil, cinnamon and thyme.

Essential Oils (EO) That Are Recommended for Meditation

Sandalwood

Sandalwood contains deep sensual properties. Its woody, sweet scent is known to soothe and comfort the body and the mind, promoting overall feelings of well-being. It is very often used as an incense and perfume.

Acts as:

- Antidepressant
- Antiseptic
- Antispasmodic
- Aphrodisiac
- Sedative
- Tonic

Blends well with:

- Lavender
- Rose
- Clove
- Geranium
- Bergamot (one of my favorites!)
- Jasmine
- Patchouli and

- Myrrh

Safety

Sandalwood is non-toxic, non-irritant, and non-sensitizing.

Patchouli

The earthy aroma of patchouli contains sedative properties that can help calm and quiet the mind. If you like light, herbal scents, patchouli will be an excellent choice.

Acts as:

- Antidepressant
- Anti-inflammatory
- Antiseptic
- Aphrodisiac
- Diuretic
- Nervine
- Nervous Stimulant
- Tonic

Blends well with:

- Vetiver
- Sandalwood
- Bergamot
- Neuroli
- Myrrh
- Rose

Safety

Patchouli is non-toxic, non-irritant and non-sensitizing.

Cedarwood

Cedarwood's sweet and mildly camphorous scent focuses the mind and relieves it of tension, anxiety and stress. It has a nice, woody touch that I personally love. Add to it some sounds of the "forest playlist" and I am in heaven! I love using cedarwood when writing as it gives me inspiration. It is with me right now actually, helping me create this book.

Acts as:

- Expectorant (helps remove mucus from the respiratory system)
- Aphrodisiac
- Nervous sedative
- Circulatory stimulant
- Tonic

Blends well with:

- Cypress
- Bergamot
- Ylang ylang (really good for meditation if you like strong, floral scents)
- Jasmine
- Rosemary
- Mimosa

Safety

It is non-toxic, non-irritant and non-sensitizing. Avoid in pregnancy (always make sure you consult your doctor, or a certified aromatherapist, or both). Keep on the safe side.

Vetiver

The distilled roots of Vetiver are known to have restorative powers. It keeps us grounded to our roots. It has a really deep woody scent with a "sweet touch". It is quite strong and persistent.

Acts as:

- Antispasmodic
- Depurative
- Nervous system sedative
- Tonic

Therefore it should not be omitted in your aroma meditation rituals.

It also helps produce red corpuscles and makes your immune system stronger.

Blends well with:

- Oakmoss
- Lavender
- Clary sage
- Violet
- Jasmine
- Mimosa

Safety

It is non-toxic, non-irritant and non-sensitizing.

Bergamot

Bergamot has a really nice sweet, yet citric scent that relaxes your body and energizes your mind. It works great in stressful situations when you need to take positive and purposeful action. This is one of my favorites, as I have already mentioned before.

Acts as:

- Natural antidepressant
- Digestive
- Stimulant
- Tonic
- Helps fights headaches and energizes

Blends well with:

- Verbena (I love it!)
- Mint
- Orange
- Lemon
- Juniper
- Chamomile
- Mandarin

Safety

It is phototoxic so if you decide to use it in dermal applications, you must avoid direct sunlight exposure, even up to 12 hours or more after application. Keep on the safe side.

Very important for aromatherapy beginners

Just like in the case of any natural therapy, if you are pregnant, lactating, on medication or suffering from any health condition, make sure you consult your physician before using aromatherapy.

Getting started

Once you have your preferred essential oil, use either a diffuser or a spray to apply the scent in your meditation area, or via self-massage as described earlier. Whatever feels right for you.

To begin with, find a quiet and peaceful place. Imagine yourself sitting in the middle of a vast clearing. Everywhere you turn, you see green. It is cool and refreshing. You can feel the dewy morning air around you.

Using your breath, bring yourself to a relaxed and peaceful state. Inhale deeply through your nose. Follow that with a long exhale through your nose. Savor and delight in the smell of your chosen essential oil. As you inhale, imagine yourself inhaling its healing and rejuvenating properties. Allow your breath to travel and flow to all parts of your body, bringing with it all the therapeutic benefits of the essential oils.

Let the scent of the essential oils envelop you and transcend you into a deeper level of relaxation and meditation.

As you drift into a meditative state, observe how your mind and body reacts to the scent that is surrounding you. Did it trigger a certain emotion and memory? Acknowledge the feelings that are prompted by this scent. Don't chase them away. Just let these emotions flow through you. Don't hold on to them. Allow these emotions to flourish and, when the time is right, be ready to let them go.

Focus yourself on the sense of smell and embrace it. Let it work for you and your other senses. Accept whatever comes to your mind. You are now focused. You focus all your attention on your amazing essential oils. Let them heal your body, mind and spirit. Let them purify your energy field. It's so easy, you just let the scents guide you. As you breathe in you feel stronger, and you let go all the negative emotions, tension and pain.

CHAPTER 6

Taste of Meditation and Relaxation:

Discover the Pleasure of Mindful Eating and Turn Your Kitchen into the Best Holistic Health Spa

Say Goodbye to Emotional and Mindless Eating...

Relaxation can also be achieved by using your sense of taste to bring your awareness to the present moment.

If you have a piece of fruit or even a piece of chocolate with you, you can take a bite before starting your meditation practice.

Sit comfortably and use your breath to relax your body. Once you find yourself in a relaxed state, start to shift your awareness to your tongue. Notice the taste of whatever it is that is inside your mouth. Pay attention to the sensations of your taste buds. Chew the food slowly and pay attention to its consistency. Observe how they react to the food that is inside your mouth. Notice how your body reacts to different kinds of food. Eat mindfully - mindful eating is one of the best skills you can develop, not only for weight loss, but also for better digestion and more energy levels.

Using your sense of taste for relaxation and meditation will help you achieve a healthy eating habit. Being mindful of your body's reactions towards certain kinds of food will remind you to choose carefully the food that you will eat.

Your body is sacred. It houses your heart and your soul. Therefore you must feed it with good food. You must be mindful of its health and well-being at all times.

Be grateful for your food. Don't take it for granted. Many people are starving and have not eaten for days or even weeks. Be grateful for water and all the amazing, nutritious foods that are helping you transform your body and mind. You deserve it.

Create your eating rituals. Before getting started on my meal, I like to use mint and chamomile essential oils in a vaporizer, as they help me feel more focused on my food. I eat slowly, and I enjoy every second of mindful eating. It's like my own holistic health spa at home.

Eating with a TV on is one of the worst habits one can develop. Luckily, now I have eliminated it from my life. Contrary to the common belief, it is not boring - it is really exciting. This is a healthy lifestyle. Do you think that a Paleolithic caveman would eat with a TV on? With so much buzz going on around Paleo Diet, and what to eat, what is not enough Paleo, what is Neo and what is Paleo - let's go back to the roots. It's not only about what you eat, but HOW you eat and HOW YOU FEEL while eating.

I hope that this can inspire you to use your eating time as your meditation and healing time. Breathe in and out. Use your imagination and go back to all the wonderful places we have visited together so far in this book. You are in control now. Meditation is yours, no matter where you are and what you do. You don't need to spend hours in a lotus pose. You can turn on your mindfulness meditation mode right now. All this can be achieved with creating a really simple, yet powerful habit. Meditate 5 minutes a day, but put your mind and soul into it.

It's not about eliminating your thoughts. It's about accepting them, embracing them and finally learning how to transform them into more empowering ones.

Whatever it is that brings you closer to your holistic wellness goals - stick to it. Reject the rest...

No time to meditate? Try to meditate while eating. Everyone needs to eat. Just like everyone needs to meditate in their own way.

To learn more about mindful eating check out my article (it's also available in audio, like most of my blog posts- my mission is to provide solutions for busy people and audio versions of my articles are perfect for those who don't have time to read long articles):

www.holisticwellnessproject.com/blog/mindfulness/mindful-eating/

CHAPTER 7

Mastering Mindfulness in a Few Easy Steps:

Forget about the Past, Focus on Now, and Create an Amazing Tomorrow

Have you ever wondered why so many people, despite all the fame, success and wealth they were able to amass through the years, still find themselves feeling anxious and depressed?

Have you ever felt that way?

There are times when you find yourself pining for things, places and people that were long gone. Other times you find yourself longing for the past to come back. There are moments when you find yourself aching for the future to come.

How many times have you blamed yourself for not doing something you should have done ages ago? How often do you find yourself wishing for things to go back to the way they were? Or how often do you find yourself drifting to the "la la land", dreaming of beautiful things to come? So many "could have beens", so many "should have beens". So many regrets. So many "what ifs". So much time wasted.

I have a confession to make, my friend. I have been that person for so many years. For a long time, I was either living in the past or in the future. I was never here, now. Until one day, I came upon an old photo of me with my family (probably around 1991) when I was a little girl aged 8. In the photo, we were all smiling and relaxing in nature. We all looked so happy and stress-free. At that time, my parents, I, and my little brother all lived in a really small and crappy apartment, yet we were all so happy. We have so many nice memories from that place really. I thought, "hmm...it makes sense" - it's not what you have, <u>but how you feel about what you have and who you are, or who you become in the process of achieving your goals that WILL actually make you happy</u>.

I looked at the picture again with fondness and tried to recall what happened that day, why we were all smiling. I ended up crying instead because, no matter how hard I tried, I just couldn't recall how I felt and what transpired during that day that made us all so happy.

All I can remember was, that during that time, while I was wearing my favorite dress, I was thinking about how good it felt to be in nature. I was there with my body, mind, and spirit. Kids know this stuff!

This is how I made a commitment to try to be grateful for <u>the now</u> and be like a little kid again - happy, here and now, exploring and enjoying.

I realized that, as an adult, or even as a teen, I wasn't really living my life. <u>I was living a lie</u>. It was all smoke and mirrors. I was either in the past or in the future, but never in the NOW.

And the life is NOW.

Not tomorrow. Not when you get a pay rise. Not when you buy a house.

Not yesterday - you see, as Tony Robbins says, "The past does not equal to future." So what's the point of dwelling on the past?

You have done something stupid? So what. We all have. What you have done is not stupid, as long as you manage to learn from it and use it to your advantage - use it to create a new, stronger you. We should learn from our mistakes and mindfulness makes us more aware of our actions and their meanings.

Embrace mindfulness.

How then do we break free from this seemingly hopeless situation? How do we begin living life and enjoying it to the fullest? The answer is quite simple, my friend. BE PRESENT. Practice mindfulness daily. Make meditation and mindfulness your life.

Mindfulness is an art and practice of consciously bringing one's awareness to the present moment, without any attachment. When in a mindful state, you are able to find peace and stillness within you. You are able to observe and acknowledge the things that are happening in the present moment, without judgment. You are simply present.

One effective way of achieving mindfulness is the practice of Five Senses Meditation, just like I taught you in this book. When meditating, you are encouraged to use breathing techniques (*pranayama*) to help you calm and quiet your mind. Though the breath should not be the main focus of the practice, it is used to guide the mind back to the present moment when it starts to wander, which normally happens during meditation.

Below are a few easy steps you can do daily to integrate a little mindfulness in your day to day activities:

- Find a quiet place. It doesn't matter where as long as there are no evident distractions like blaring TVs and lit computers. Try to do an occasional technology detox.

- Sit comfortably. There is no specific sitting pose to take here. The key is for you to be comfortable. Crossing your legs is one of the easiest ways to seat comfortably. Lengthen your spine but don't overdo. Sit tall, not rigidly. Keep your neck long and soft, and your sit bone grounded to the earth.

o Once you find your seat, you may gently close your eyes if you want to or simply let your gaze fall upon whatever is in front of you. Don't strain your eyes. Don't force it to focus on one object. Let your eyes rest on any object that is before you.

o Observe your breath. Follow it as it goes in and out of your nostrils. Don't try to control and manipulate it. Let it flow naturally. Just pay attention the rise and fall of your chest. Don't try to hold it. Breathing is an organic and natural process. Let it flow through you the way it should be.

o As you breathe, slowly bring your awareness to the present moment. Use any of your five senses to bring mindfulness into your practice. You can start with your sense of sight, by observing the things around you. Then move on and gently shift your focus to the sounds around you. After a while, bring your attention to the smell, taste and feel of your surroundings. There is no prescribed order. Find what feels good, and right, and go from there.

You will find thoughts wandering from time to time. That's okay. When that happens don't judge yourself. Don't feel bad about it. You didn't do anything wrong. Your mind is doing what it usually does. Acknowledge that you've been thinking. Accept what just happened, and then gently bring your awareness back to the present moment. Use your breath and any of your five senses to guide you back.

Incorporating mindfulness and meditation in my life has greatly helped me regain some of the time I have lost pining and longing for the past, and for the future. I was able to bring my focus and awareness back to the present. With a quiet mind, I was able to let intuition and insight flow freely into my consciousness and awareness. This has helped me find my passion and create a balanced lifestyle. Now, it is my mission to inspire thousands of people throughout the world to do the same. It all comes down to embracing natural therapy, such as, in this case, mindful meditation and use it to work on your body, mind, emotions, and spirit.

The act of being mindful has opened my eyes to the blessings that I already had. I became more grateful. I became kinder, more loving and more compassionate to the people around me and, most of all, to myself. I found light and happiness, wherever life takes me. From there on, things began to change for the good.

My new, empowering belief I am cultivating now is that every person, every human being, can teach you something amazing, even if you don't resonate with them 100%. This belief has helped me realize how bad it is for my soul to judge other people. *It also feels bad to be judged, right?*

Of course, it is still a journey for me, I am not perfect. I go for progress.

Without any judgment and attachment, I now look at the past with fondness, and look forward to the future with confidence, security and abundance. You can do the same, just following what I am teaching you in this book and on my blog – www.holisticwellnessproject.com

CHAPTER 8

Walking Meditation:

Bring Joy and Peace in an Active Way and Discover the Body & Mind Connection

Meditation in action is one of the best ways to describe walking meditation. This type of meditation will allow you to use your experience of walking to bring focus and awareness to yourself and the present moment. It will also let you use your five senses to help bring mindfulness into your practice. It will work great for those who say that meditation is boring, they can't sit still or can't focus. Move your body then! Active meditation is really miraculous for your overall health and well-being.

One of my favorite places for meditation near where I live...

Let me guide you through the practice with these simple and easy instructions to follow:

Let us begin by finding an open space, preferably in nature. Enter that open space and stand there. Just stand for a few minutes and be aware. Notice the weight of your body on the soles of your feet. Pay attention to the ground beneath you. Notice how your body moves ever so slightly to be able to sustain your upright position and balance. Many times we take for granted the ability to stand on the ground. We forgot how we tried so hard as babies to stand up. It took us about a year or so to be able to do this. Some people would even give anything just for them to be able to stand on their feet. Be grateful for this gift. Acknowledge and enjoy it.

Once you find yourself firmly grounded, begin to walk. You don't need to walk slowly. Just follow your normal pace. You don't need to manipulate and control your movements. Don't try to change them either. Just be aware of your movements. Pay attention to your body.

Pay attention to your feet. Be mindful of every step that you take. Notice how your heel touches the ground first, and feel as your feet shift and roll the weight onto the balls of your feet. Feel the energy flow through the soles of your feet. Notice the pattern that your feet follow. Left, right, left, right.

From your feet, slowly shift your focus towards your ankles. Notice the sensations in the joints. Feel the tension and release every time you lift your foot in the air and then allow it to touch the ground. Relax your joints by finding lightness in every step you take.

Be aware of your legs and your knees. Notice how the muscles flex and relax every time you take a step. Pay attention to the heat that each movement brings to your body. Be mindful of your knees. Notice how the joints move smoothly without a hitch. Feel the sensations as you continue to take a step forward.

Continue to bring your focus up to your pelvis. Pay attention to the sensation of being connected from the ground to the soles of your feet, to your legs and up to your hips. You are one with the ground and the earth. Let your awareness travel up to your spine. Notice its movement, as you step one foot in front of the other. Observe how it slightly sways from side to side, gently twisting from left to right and right to left. Savor this gentle twist as it gently releases tension in your body.

Notice your core. Pay attention to the muscles that are working double time to hold your body up. Observe how your abdominal muscles contract from time to time. Feel your chest expanding every time you take a step forward. Notice your arms gently swaying and falling into their own rhythm as you continue to walk at your own pace.

Move your focus to your neck. Keep it long and soft. Notice how you tilt your head from one side to another, and be mindful of the changes in your perspective as your head shifts from one angle to another.

As you are walking, thoughts and emotions will arise. Simply acknowledge the flow and ebb of these feelings. Don't chase them away, but don't hang on to them either. Simply let them be. These thoughts and feelings are a part of you. Accept them for what they are, without judgment.

Finally, relax your jaws and your eyes. Relax your eyelids. Don't strain your sight. Don't chase the horizon. Let it fall upon you. Simply let yourself walk. Take one step at a time and enjoy the journey.

Once you've reached your destination, allow yourself to come to a stop. Do it gently. Savor the feeling of standing still. Notice the solid ground under the soles of your feet. Stand quietly and calmly. Experience yourself in this moment and try to listen to the callings of your soul and the Universe.

ADDITIONAL RESOURCES:

www.holisticwellnessproject.com/blog/mindfulness/

CONCLUSION

DISCOVERING BODY-MIND-SPIRIT CONNECTION AND EMBRACING HOLISTIC WELLNESS

Thank you again for purchasing my book. It really means a lot to me.

I am happy that you have managed to keep an open mind as you read through this book and learned how to you use your five senses in bringing your awareness to the present moment.

When your mind is quiet and still, you allow yourself to see clearly, to hear the truth, to taste the goodness, to smell life and to feel love. To find peace and calmness inside you is to allow yourself to listen and heed the callings of your heart, your soul and of the Universe.

Give yourself the gift of living in the present moment. Let go of the past and don't hang on to the future. Acknowledge what you have now and pay attention to it. Be grateful. Open your heart and your mind. Allow the light to flow inside you. Allow yourself to enjoy the journey of your life.

The practice of meditation and mindfulness is simply an act of noticing. It is a conscious effort of bringing your awareness to the present moment. When you are in the present moment, you become mindful of the things that are happening inside and around you. You allow yourself to experience life as it happens right before you. You don't judge. You don't get attached. You are simply letting things be.

One more thing...I might need your help!

If you enjoyed this book and received value from it, could you please share your experience with other readers? One sentence review on Amazon is enough, and it will surely make my day and help me create more holistic resources for you and your wellbeing.

If there is something you don't understand, have questions, suggestions, and/or doubts, **please make sure you talk to me first**. Simply e-mail me at: info@holisticwellnessproject.com

I am here to help!

As I bring this book to an end, I wish all these, from my heart to yours:

May you notice that you are blessed with so much.

May you notice that you are loved.

May you notice that you are happy.

May you notice that you are beautiful.

May you notice that you are kind.

May you notice that you are wise.

May you notice that you are perfect.

May you notice that the Divine is in you.

May you notice that you are alive.

Let go of your destination and enjoy your journey in life.

Let's keep in touch!

For more inspiration, articles, books, eBooks, audiobooks and podcasts visit the blog:

www.HolisticWellnessProject.com

www.holisticwellnessproject.com/books

www.amazon.com/author/mtuchowska

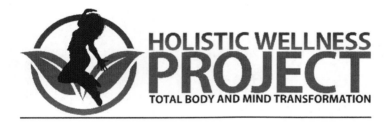

Finally, let's connect!

www.facebook.com/HolisticWellnessProject

www.twitter.com/Marta_Wellness

www.instagram.com/Marta_Wellness

ABOUT MARTA TUCHOWSKA

Marta Tuchowska is a passionate holistic wellness coach and author on a mission. She wants to help you create a healthy body, mind and spirit through a balanced lifestyle. Marta has a strong background in healing and health (certified in massage therapy, holistic nutrition, aromatherapy and Reiki), and she infuses her natural therapy knowledge with motivational and practical life coaching as well as NLP to help you create a life full of energy, health and happiness. Marta wants to make it easy, doable and fun. She calls it holistic lifestyle design for modern, 21st-century, busy folks! Join the exciting journey of total body and mind transformation at: www.HolisticWellnessProject.com

Free Gifts from Marta:

Don't forget to download your free audiobook: *Mindfulness for Busy People:*

Download Link:

www.holisticwellnessproject.com/mindfulness

As an added bonus, you will also receive these:

81264097R00040

Made in the USA
Middletown, DE
22 July 2018